IF YOU WERE A...

Construction Worker

IF YOU WERE A...
Construction Worker

Virginia Schomp

BENCHMARK BOOKS

MARSHALL CAVENDISH
NEW YORK

The big bucket on this backhoe can scoop up tons of rocks and dirt.

If you were a construction worker, you would make things grow. Not grass or flowers but bridges and tunnels and buildings that reach to the sky.

Watch your step! It's dangerous up there on a growing skyscraper. Cover your ears! This backhoe makes an enormous hole . . . and a stupendous noise.

What will rise from the hole? A house? An amusement park? A space shuttle launch pad? You could help make all these things grow if you were a construction worker.

High above ground, construction workers place the steel beams of a new skyscraper.

An excavator dumps broken rock cleared from the foundation hole.

Workers pour concrete to make the foundation for the new building.

Backhoes bite the earth. Construction workers are digging a hole for a building foundation. Buildings that sit on strong foundations won't sink into the ground.

This foundation must be very strong. It will carry the weight of a skyscraper. After the hole is dug, workers will hammer piles—long steel and concrete blocks— deep into the solid rock below the ground. Like the roots of a tree, the piles will keep the tall building steady and straight.

When the ground is too hard for the backhoes to dig, a jackhammer pounds it to pieces.

A superintendent directs the workers, making sure they do their jobs right.

Have you ever built a tower out of Popsicle sticks? Many steel skyscrapers are put together the same way. The sticks standing straight up are called columns. The sticks that connect the columns are called girders.

Construction workers attach columns to the tops of the foundation piles. Then they connect girders to the columns. They attach steel floor beams to the girders and lay planks over the beams so they can walk around.

The first floor is finished. Up goes another column, and the second floor starts to grow.

This skyscraper is made from concrete columns and slabs instead of steel.

Fifty floors, sixty floors, seventy. Higher and higher the skyscraper climbs. The men and women wrestling all that steel into place are called ironworkers. Some days their work takes them to the clouds.

If you were an ironworker, you would plant your feet on a narrow beam. On the street far below, the people look like ants. Around you is open space—no walls, no floors. Only your safety belt and a good sense of balance keep you safe.

Each step is dangerous, but this ironworker makes it look easy.

Stone blocks will cover the sides of this skyscraper.

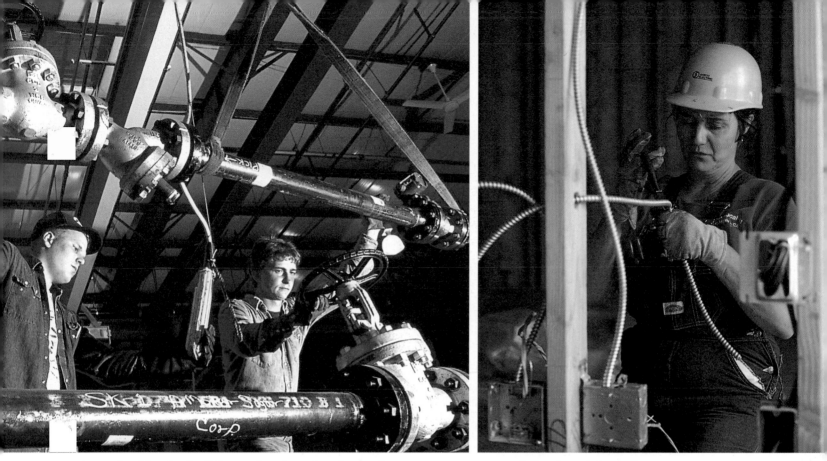

Inside the building, plumbers hook up pipes to carry water, while electricians fit up wires and boxes to carry electricity.

As the ironworkers hurry skyward, other construction workers follow right behind. Some cover the outside of the building with stone, metal, or glass. Others pour concrete for the ceilings and floors. Plumbers place pipes. Electricians install wires. Carpenters hammer at walls and doors. Thousands of workers doing dozens of different jobs will help take this skyscraper to the top.

It takes years to build a skyscraper, months to build a house. But in some ways, the work is very much the same.

If you were building a house, you would start with a strong foundation. Beams of wood give your building shape and strength.

Carpenters build the frame of the house, then cover it with sheets of wood.

hat happens when
d must cross over
er, a gap in moun-
, or another busy
? Construction
kers build a bridge.
his bridge rests on
huge towers set in
foundations under
water. Steel cables
ch from the tops of
towers to hold up
bridge's roadway.
rkers began building
roadway from
posite ends of the
dge. One day soon
ey will meet in the
iddle.

In just a few weeks, this bridge in Canada will be ready for travelers.

A tool called a level shows if floors are straight.

The plumber runs pipes under the floors and through the walls.

Like a skyscraper, your house needs teamwork to grow. Carpenters, electricians, painters, plumbers, roofers—many hands must work together to turn a wooden skeleton into a home.

To build a highway, construction workers use cement mixers, cranes, bulldozers, trucks, and other heavy machines.

What connects our homes and skyscrapers, our cities and towns? Millions of miles of crisscrossing roads.

These construction workers are building a new road. First, earthmoving machines must clear the way. Bulldozers rip up bushes, and scrapers slice through hillsides. Compactors pack down dirt with their heavy rollers.

When the ground is flat and hard, tru of crushed stone. Then a noisy machine paver spreads hot black asphalt (AS-faw who rake smooth that sticky mix of tar a the hottest, smelliest job of all!

Workers smooth the asphalt dropped onto the new road by the p

This jumbo has drills that attack the rock in five places at once.

Building a bridge over high mountains is hard and expensive. Sometimes the road must go *through* the mountains instead.

How would you dig a tunnel through solid rock? You might use a special drilling machine called a jumbo. Where the rock is too hard to drill, you would make small holes and fill them with dynamite. You'll want to be far away when you hear that boom!

What other kinds of structures do construction workers build? The list includes schools and hospitals, shopping malls and sports arenas, shipyards and airports and nuclear power plants.

A web of steel rods will make the walls of this water treatment plant strong.

A welder repairs an underwater oil well.

If you were a construction worker, you might hang from a cliff to build a dam across a river. In a diver's suit, you could work underwater, repairing an oil-drilling rig. Someday you might even blast off with the astronauts to help build a space station far above the earth.

It took a long time to build this apartment house, but only a minute to bring it down.

When the wrecking ball hits, places that used to be inside *are suddenly* outside.

When is a construction worker a *destruction* worker? When there's a building to be *un*built.

Workers may use a wrecking ball swinging from a truck crane to smash the building bit by bit. Some buildings are too tall and tough to bring down this way. Workers must carefully place explosives in the lower floors. One giant blast and the whole building collapses in a cloud of smoke and dust.

Dump trucks haul away the pieces. Now there's an empty patch of land all ready for a brand-new building.

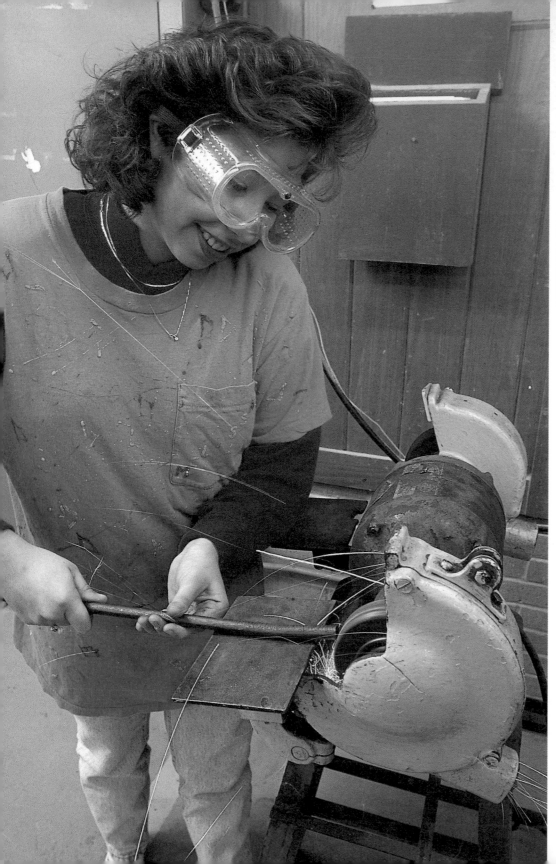

Training programs teach students how to safely use construction tools—from grinders and sanders to hammers and power saws.

Would you like to make a building rise from an empty lot? If you don't mind hard work with some danger and excitement mixed in, you could be a construction worker.

Most construction workers start as apprentices. They help out a skilled worker who teaches them a job. Many apprentices also go to training school to learn how to make things grow.

What would your hands help raise? A cozy new home? A graceful bridge? Or will you build a tower that scrapes the sky?

CONSTRUCTION IN TIME

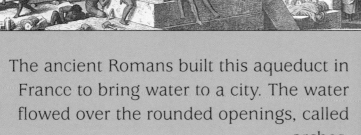

The pyramids of ancient Egypt, built from huge blocks of stone, were some of the earliest "skyscrapers."

The ancient Romans built this aqueduct in France to bring water to a city. The water flowed over the rounded openings, called arches.

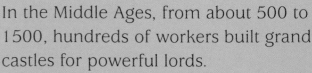

In the Middle Ages, from about 500 to 1500, hundreds of workers built grand castles for powerful lords.

George Washington helped plan the U.S. Capitol building in Washington, D.C. Workers rebuilt the Capitol after the British burned it down during the War of 1812.

When the 984-foot Eiffel Tower rose in Paris, France, in 1889, it was the tallest building in the world.

In 1931, the 102-story Empire State Building, in New York City, took the title of tallest. Today it's the fifth-highest building in the world.

29

A CONSTRUCTION WORKER'S CLOTHING AND TOOLS

Clothes give protection—a hard hat for the head, safety goggles for the eyes, leather gloves for the hands, boots with nonskid soles for the feet.

A construction worker's tools might include . . . hammers, screwdrivers, wrenches, saws, a power drill . . .

. . . a power saw for cutting . . .

. . . a jackhammer for drilling rock and pavement.

WORDS TO KNOW

apprentice Someone who works alongside an older, experienced worker to learn how to do a job.

column A steel or concrete block placed vertically—standing up—in a building.

foundation The underground structure on which a building sits.

girder A steel beam used to connect a building's columns.

ironworker A construction worker who puts together buildings made of steel. Ironworkers got their name two hundred years ago, when large buildings had floor beams made of iron.

piles Steel or concrete columns hammered into the ground as part of a building foundation.

welder A construction worker who uses heat to melt and join metal.

This book is for our Texas trio, Joey, Vinnie, and Gary

Benchmark Books
Marshall Cavendish Corporation
99 White Plains Road
Tarrytown, New York 10591

Library of Congress Cataloging-in-Publication Data
Schomp, Virginia, date.
If you were a—construction worker / Virginia Schomp.
p. cm. Includes index.
Summary: Describes the tools and skills that construction workers need to build houses, bridges, and other structures.
!SBN 0-7614-0617-4 (lib. bdg.)
1. Building—Juvenile literature. 2. Construction workers—Juvenile literature. [1. Construction workers. 2. Occupations.] I. Title.
TH149.S36 1998   624—dc21   96-51537 CIP AC

Photo research by Debbie Needleman

Front cover: *The Image Bank*, Barros & Barros

The photographs in this book are used by permission and through the courtesy of: *The Picture Cube*: John Yurka, 1; Ken Kaminsky, 6; J.D. Sloan, 15 (left); Robert Finken, 24; Henryk T. Kaiser, 30 (top right). *Henry Horenstein*: 2, 7 (left and right). *Westlight*: Walter Hodges, 4-5; Fotografia Productions, 31. *The Image Works*: Michael Okoniewski, 5; David Wells, 12 (left); Frank Pedrick, 22; Bob Collins, 30 (center). *PhotoEdit*: Dana White, 8; A. Ramey, 13 (right); Dennis MacDonald, 15 (right); Mark Richards, 27 (left and right). *Robert Frerck/Odyssey Productions/Chicago*: 9, 16, 28 (middle). *The Image Bank*: Don Carrol, 10; Francesco Ruggeri, 12-13 (center); Grant V. Faint, 18-19; H.J. Burkard, 20; David W. Hamilton, 29 (top); Anthony Boccaccio, 30 (bottom right). *Photo Researchers*: Andy Levin, 11. *Bill Sciallo*: 14. *Uniphoto Picture Agency*: Les Moore, 17; Royce Bair, 25. *Central Artery Project, Boston*: Andy Ryan, 21; Louis Martin, 30 (left). *Ken Graham Agency*: Mark Dionne, 23. *Stock Boston*: Bob Daemmrich, 26 (left); Rob Nelson, 26 (right). *Index, Barcelona/The Bridgeman Art Library, London*: 28 (top). *Bibliotheque Nationale, Paris/Bridgeman Art Library, London*: 28 (bottom). *Mary Evans Picture Library*: 29 (bottom left). *Archive Photos*: 29 (bottom right).

Printed in the United States of America
1 3 5 7 8 6 4 2

INDEX